Yorkshire Dales: **Mysterious Walks**

AF007686

First published in 2025 by:

Northern Eye Books Limited
Northern Eye Books, Tattenhall, Cheshire CH3 9PX

© Northern Eye Books Limited 2025

ISBN 978-1-914589-23-2

Text: *Frank Kew*

Series editor: *Tony Bowerman*

Photographs: *Neil Bland, Frank Kew, Adobe Stock, iStock, Shutterstock, Dreamstime*

Design: *Carl Rogers and Laura Hodgkinson*

Frank Kew has asserted his rights under the Copyright, Designs and Patents Act, 1988 to be identified as the author of this work. All rights reserved.

A CIP catalogue record for this book is available from the British Library.

Cover: *The Idol Stone, Brimham (Walk 2)*

Photo: Neil Bland

www.northerneyebooks.co.uk

 @northerneyebooks

 @northerneyeboo

 @northerneyebooks

For sales enquiries, please call 01928 723 744
tony@northerneyebooks.co.uk

Important Advice: The routes described in this book are undertaken at the reader's own risk. Walkers should take into account their level of fitness, wear suitable footwear and clothing, and carry food and water. It is also advisable to take the relevant OS map with you in case you get lost and leave the area covered by our maps.

Whilst every care has been taken to ensure the accuracy of the route directions, the publishers cannot accept responsibility for errors or omissions, or for changes in the details given. Nor can the publisher and copyright owners accept responsibility for any consequences arising from the use of this book.

If you find any inaccuracies in either the text or maps, please write or email us at the address above. Thank you.

This book contains mapping data licensed from the Ordnance Survey with the permission of the Controller of Her Majesty's Stationery Office. © Crown copyright 2025 All rights reserved. Licence number AC0000833184

Contents

The Yorkshire Dales National Park 4
Top 10 Walks: Mysterious Walks 6
1 | **Hoffman kiln** & **Catrigg Force** 8
2 | **Brimham** - *'Rock of Ages'* 14
3 | **Swinsty Hall** & **Timble Gill** 20
4 | **Hackfall Woods' follies** 26
5 | **Knights Templar in Wensleydale** 32
6 | **Scoska Cave** & **Littondale** 38
7 | **Druids' Temple** & **Lobley Hall** 42
8 | **Ancient 'rock art' on Ilkley Moor** 48
9 | **Nine Standards Rigg** 54
10 | **Elbolton Cave** - *Hill of the Dead* 58
Useful Information 64

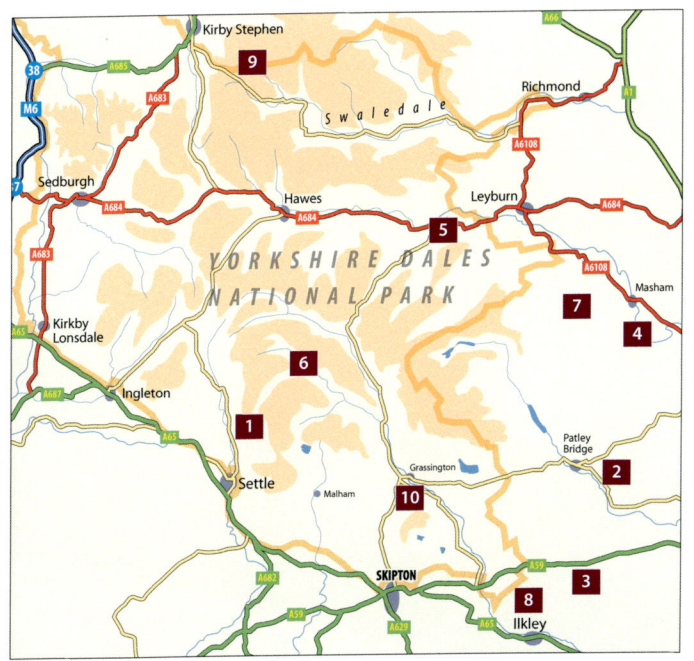

The Yorkshire Dales National Park

CREATED IN 1954, THE YORKSHIRE DALES NATIONAL PARK covers 2,178 square kilometres/841 square miles of the central Pennines. As well as some of Yorkshire's most magnificent landscapes, the National Park also includes parts of historic Lancashire and Westmorland such as the Orton and Howgill Fells and the Lune Valley. Upwards of 8 million visitors a year enjoy this striking countryside with its picturesque stone villages.

The 'Dales' is something of a misnomer, for in addition to the beautiful dales, the area incorporates great tracts of wild moorland, the famous 'Three Peaks', and an intriguing industrial heritage. Over 1,300 miles of rights of way allow walkers to explore all aspects of the Park. What's more, almost 11,000 hectares of 'open access' land provides boundless possibilities for exploring this heady mix of limestone and gritstone scenery.

The enigmatic Nine Standards Rigg

Mysteries of the Yorkshire Dales

Since the last Ice Age, hunter-gatherers, then farmers of crops and animals, then miners, have moved into the Dales and made their mark on the landscape. From prehistoric standing stones and rock art, to lonely wayside crosses, monastic routes, packhorse bridges, medieval churches and shrines. More recently, there are follies in parkland and relics of the extraction of limestone, copper and lead.

The land too holds mysteries, from fantastical wind-sculpted gritstone edges to the forbidding, dark liminal spaces of caves —once thought to provide portals to a veiled netherworld.

A rich folklore attests to beliefs in fantastical creatures such as kelpies, trolls, fairies and witches, peopling untamed uplands or the cavernous underworld. All give rise to …

"…the ghosts of the region's past (and)…those spirits of place which give the landscape its unique magic and fascination."

— Phil Smith

TOP 10 Walks: Mysterious Walks

THIS CURIOUS LITTLE BOOK IS INTENDED TO INSPIRE AND INFORM an exploration of the Yorkshire Dales' unexpected oddities and mysteries. Each walk visits at least one—either natural phenomenon such as rocks or caves, or bizarre man-made features—some of which defy explanation whilst attracting wild or weird theories. Where relevant, local folklore and strange tales are included as well. Naturally, no walk is complete without a restorative cuppa or pint, so details of watering holes are provided too.

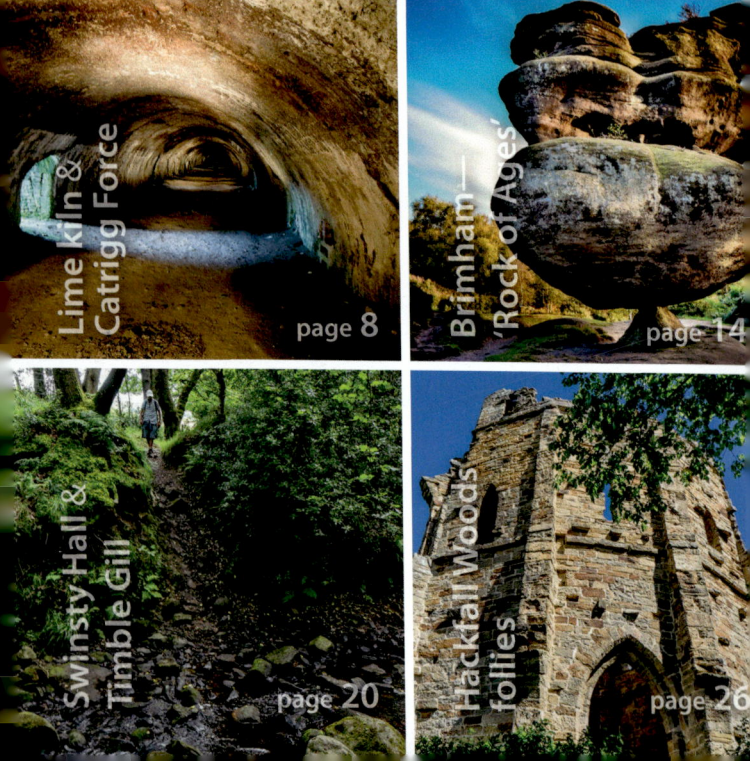

Lime Kiln & Catrigg Force — page 8

Brimham — 'Rock of Ages' — page 14

Swinsty Hall & Timble Gill — page 20

Hackfall Woods follies — page 26

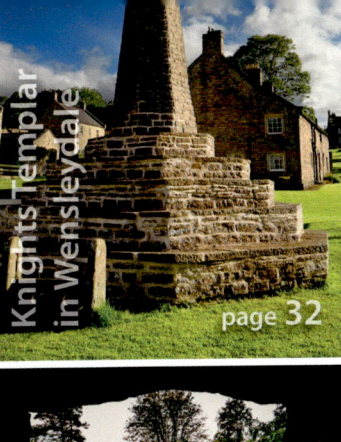
Knights Templar in Wensleydale — page 32

Scoska Cave & Littondale — page 38

Druids' Temple & Lobley Hall — page 42

Ancient rock art on Ilkley Moor — page 48

Nine Standards Rigg — page 54

Elbolton Cave - Hill of the Dead — page 58

Sunlight filters into the chambers of the Hoffman Kiln

walk 1

Hoffman Kiln & Catrigg Force
Kilns, waterfalls, and pavements: a walk shaped by limestone

What to expect:
One ascent and descent, mainly field paths and some moorland with long-distance views

Distance/time: 8 kilometres/5 miles. Allow 3-3 ½ hours

Start: Stainforth village carpark (fee) BD24 9PF

Grid ref: SD 820 672

Ordnance Survey Map: OL2 Yorkshire Dales Southern & Western areas *Whernside, Ingleborough, and Pen-y-ghent*

After the Walk: The Craven Heifer, Main Road, Stainforth BD24 9PB
01729 822435 | www.cravenheiferstainforth.co.uk

Walk outline
From the ancient village of Stainforth, the walk climbs the fellside following the Pennine Bridleway, before visiting the atmospheric waterfall of Catrigg Force. Returning to the open fell and a Nature Reserve, there are spectacular views towards the famous Three Peaks, before a lovely stroll descending through farmland to the outskirts of the hamlet of Langcliffe. The return takes in Stainforth Scar and the spectacular Hoffman Kiln. The walk can be extended to Stainforth Force.

Hoffman Lime Kiln
Scattered throughout the limestone dales are pre-industrial field kilns used for agricultural purposes to 'sweeten' the land, and for building mortar. Nothing, however, approached the size and capacity of Hoffman Kilns, this one being built in 1873 for the Craven Lime Works Company and having 22 chambers which were fired in sequence. Sited here because of the good source of limestone and being adjacent to the Settle-Carlisle Railway, it was operational until 1937. It is one of the best preserved in the country, missing only its brick chimney which collapsed in the 1950s.

Hoffman kiln

Leaping salmon

10 ♦ TOP 10 WALKS **YORKSHIRE DALES: Mysterious Walks**

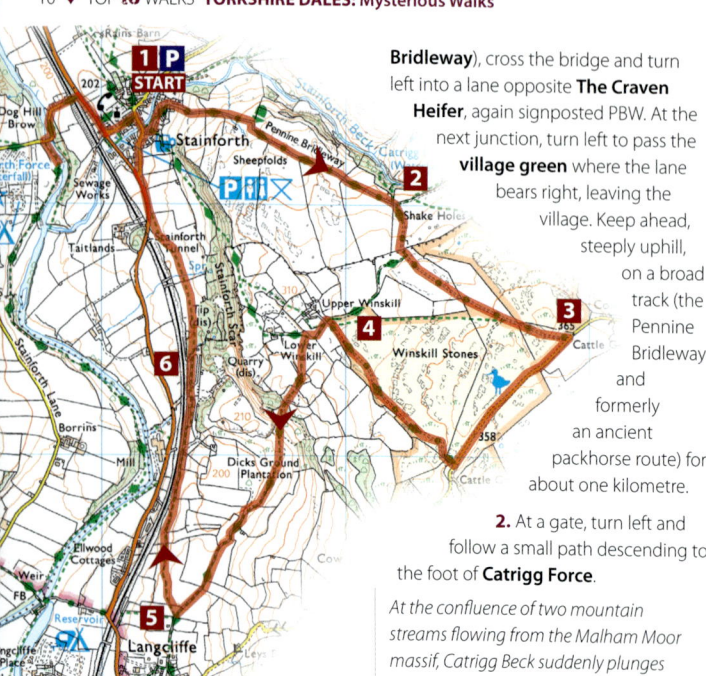

Bridleway), cross the bridge and turn left into a lane opposite **The Craven Heifer**, again signposted PBW. At the next junction, turn left to pass the **village green** where the lane bears right, leaving the village. Keep ahead, steeply uphill, on a broad track (the Pennine Bridleway and formerly an ancient packhorse route) for about one kilometre.

2. At a gate, turn left and follow a small path descending to the foot of **Catrigg Force**.

At the confluence of two mountain streams flowing from the Malham Moor massif, Catrigg Beck suddenly plunges into Stainforth Beck within a steep-sided, magical and mysterious wooded gorge, studded with limestone slabs and ancient gnarled trees. This is a hidden gem and, understandably, was a favourite destination for the composer Edward Elgar when he stayed with his friend, Dr Buck, in Settle.

Retrace your steps back uphill to go through the gate, and follow the broad track to the right. At the next gate, bear left and keep ahead on a broad track

The Walk

1. Turn right out of the car park and walk into the village. At the road junction, turn right signposted 'PBW' (**Pennine**

Walk 1 – **Hoffman Kiln** & **Catrigg Force** ♦ 11

The magical gorge of Catrigg Force on a summer's day

for 700 metres to meet a small tarmac road, the highest point of the walk at 365 metres above sea level.

3. Turn right down the road for about 750 metres and turn right into **Winskill Stones Nature Reserve**, an area of limestone pavement, passing **Samson's Toe**, a huge boulder on the right (see below).

Bought by Plantlife International, the Reserve is dedicated to Geoff Hamilton, the well-known gardener, who was concerned that the limestone was being robbed out for people's rockeries. There are great views across the Ribble Valley towards Ingleborough (723 metres), Pen-y-ghent (694 metres), and Whernside (736 metres).

4. At the end of the reserve, turn left at a path junction towards '**Lower Winskill**'. Before the farm, turn left over a stile signposted 'Langcliffe'. The path descends steeply through scattered woodland known as **Dicks Ground Plantation** into a shallow valley to the south of the imposing limestone cliff of **Stainforth Scar**, becoming a **green lane** between field walls. Before entering **Langcliffe**, and just before a small allotment, turn

The ruins of Hoffman Kiln settle into the woodland under Stainforth Scar

right over a stile signposted 'Stainforth 1¼ miles'.

5. The way ahead across fields gradually descends to run alongside the **Settle-Carlisle railway line**. Cross a small lane by a bridge and climb some steps to reach a newly-built commercial complex. Keep ahead between the buildings, to where the footpath restarts, and arrive at the **Hoffman Kiln**.

Limestone mixed with coal was stacked into each kiln and one was set alight with additional coal added through the roof vents to keep it burning. Flues regulated the heat and speed of burn, and smoke was carried away through the chimney. As one chamber burnt, the next two or three warmed up in readiness for burning. Behind the burn, lime cooled down, was shovelled out and loaded onto railway wagons in a nearby siding. On average, it took six weeks for all the limestone in the circuit of 22 kilns to be burned.

6. Passing the kiln on the right, the path continues up steps and over a small beck. Bear right as indicated and leave the **Stainforth Scar woodland**. Keep ahead across two fields where the path meets the **B6479** Settle/Stainforth road. Turn right and after 100m, bear right to enter the village passing **The Craven Heifer Inn** to reach the village car park.

To visit **Stainforth Force waterfall**, pass the car park and turn right onto the main road. After 200 metres, turn left onto a narrow lane which crosses the river on an ancient packhorse bridge. *In autumn, the falls just below the bridge are a great place to watch Atlantic salmon leaping on their way to spawn upstream.* Re-trace your steps to the car park to complete the walk. ♦

Samson's Toe

This glacial 'erratic' in the Winskill Stones Reserve, at SD 832 663, was deposited by retreating ice flows around 12,000 years ago at the end of the last Ice Age. It has no relation to the local geology, being made of 'greywacke', a mixture of pebbles, quartz, and feldspar, possibly originating in the Lake District. But legend has it that Samson broke off his toe here, in an effort to jump across the valley.

The effects of thousands of years of erosion at Brimham

walk 2

Brimham—'Rock of Ages'

Fantastical rocks—shaped by geology or the Druids?

What to expect: Moorland, farmland and country lanes with one steady climb

Distance/time: 7 kilometres/4 miles. Allow 3½ - 4 hours

Start: National Trust Carpark (fee) at Brimham Rocks - HG3 4DW

Grid ref: SE 206 650

Ordnance Survey Map: OS Explorer 298 Nidderdale *Fountains Abbey, Ripon and Pateley Bridge*

After the Walk: The Half-Moon Inn, Fellbeck, Pateley Bridge, Harrogate HG3 5ET | www.half-moon.co.uk | 01423 711560

Walk outline

After a visit to most of the rock formations and the Visitor Centre, the route heads eastwards across moorland to reach the Nidderdale Way and leave the Brimham estate. The middle part of the walk is a circular ramble through lush farmland, initially following a medieval track bordering the monastic estate of Fountains Abbey, then visiting a C17th lodge, and the hamlet of Walsill. The return is a steady climb to re-cross Brimham Moor back to the car park.

Brimham Rocks

Brimham is a weird and wonderful natural landscape of strangely-shaped outcrops of millstone grit, now providing panoramic views over Nidderdale. Laid down in a braided river system some 300 million years ago, the area was later lifted up by plate tectonics associated with the formation of the Pennines. Successive Ice Ages wore away the softer rock leaving fantastical shapes; erosion by ice, wind, and rain continues to this day. These geological and environmental processes over eons of time were only understood in the C20th. Earlier, eminent antiquarians believed that the rocks were shaped by the Druids.

'Druids' writing desk

Red grouse

The Walk

1. Pick up an information leaflet from the **National Trust office** in the car park. Then take the flight of steps to the left of the main path signposted as the 'scenic route', marked in red on the leaflet.

This passes some amazingly-shaped rock outcrops with names such as 'Smartie Tube', 'Eagle', and 'Cannon Rocks'.

On approaching the **Visitor Centre and Café**, turn left on the main track, marked in blue on the leaflet. Complete the circular blue route, passing the 'Dancing Bear', 'Druids Writing Desk' and the 'Idol' rocks amongst others to arrive back at the Visitor Centre (worth a visit).

The Visitor Centre was built in 1792 by Lord Grantley as a hunting lodge and 'for the accommodation of visitors'. By 1838, Rock House as it was then named, provided 'tea, coffee or luncheon…lemonade, ginger beer and cigars..hay and stabling for horses'. Now called Brimham House, the National Trust acquired the estate in 1970, currently attracting over 200,000 visitors a year.

© Crown copyright and/or database right. All rights reserved. Licence number AC0000833184

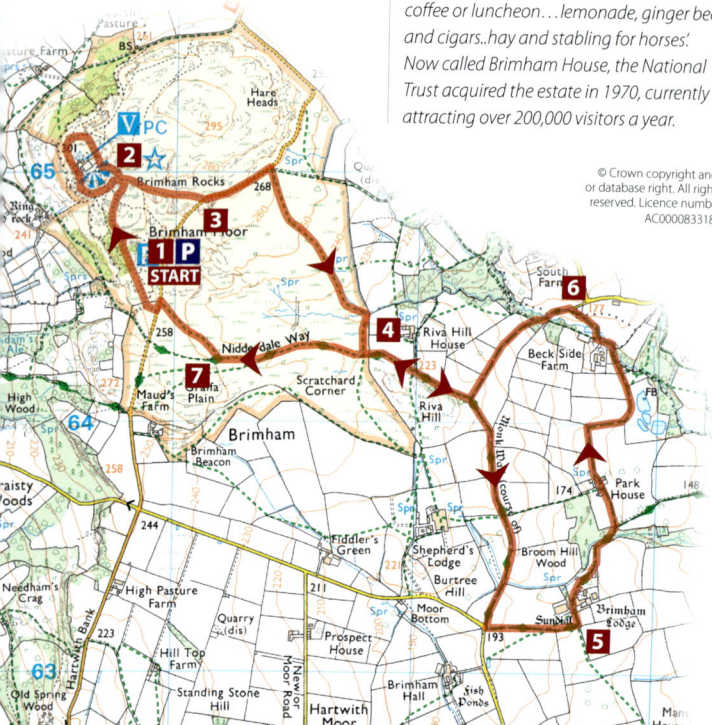

Walk 2 – **Brimham**—'Rock of Ages'

The Idol Stone balances on the most improbable base

2. From the Visitor Centre, retrace your steps on the main path for about 75 metres back to the rock marked on the map as No. 17, 'Flower Pot'. Turn left and, after another 75 metres, turn right to initially follow a fence on the left. The route is very braided due to the large footfall in the area, but keep to the left of No.19, 'Middle Crags', and continue to the road, with the fence on your left.

3. Turn left on the road and continue for about 300 metres, ignoring all stiles to the left or right. At a dip in the road and a turn-off marked as 'Private Road', turn right to take the signposted path through a metal gate. The way ahead descends gradually across **flat moorland**, boggy in places, and crosses a **footbridge** next to a wall on the left. Soon after, arrive at a path junction. Turn left to cross a stile and leave the **Brimham Rocks National Trust estate**.

The route has now joined the **Nidderdale Way**, *a 68-mile circular route to the head of Nidderdale and back.*

4. At the next gate, pass **Riva Hill House** off to the left, and keep ahead until the tarmac track bears left. Bear right through

Evening sun bathes the rock escarpment at Brimham

a farm gate and keep ahead, generally southwards, for about 1 kilometre until the path meets a road.

This is a medieval track, following 'The Monk Wall', part of a boundary of the extensive estate owned by Fountains Abbey until the dissolution of the monasteries by Henry VIII in the 1530s. By 1252, Fountains Abbey owned the whole of the Brimham Rocks area using it as pasture for their sheep.

At the road, turn left, eastwards, onto the track leading to **Brimham Lodge**, built in 1661 and now a farmhouse. On approaching the farm, take the left-hand fork to pass in front of farm sheds.

5. At the end of the sheds and just before Brimham Lodge (worth a visit), turn left to walk behind Brimham Lodge and descend to cross a **stream** and then keep ahead to pass **Park House** on the left.

The way ahead swings right and then left, passing some attractive man-made lakes on the right, to arrive at **Beck Side Farm**. Keep ahead to pass an old **millpond**, ascending to a lane at **Warsill Parish Hall**.

6. Turn left down the lane to cross **Thornton Beck** before climbing steadily to swing right and rejoin the **Nidderdale Way**. Re-pass **Riva Hill House**, this time on the right, and keep ahead to re-enter the **Brimham Rocks National Trust area**. Keep ahead, westwards, on the **Nidderdale Way** and, at a fork, bear right keeping to the main track.

7. After another 100 metres, bear right off the main track and continue across the heath, to arrive at a metal gate and then the road. Turn left and then right, back to the **NT car park** to complete the walk. ♦

Ancient Druids

In 1844, a list of 'British Monuments commonly called Druidical' included the rocks at Brimham. One antiquarian wrote… 'fragments of rock obtained great regard, even veneration from people of great antiquity: here they are found placed one on another, some have plainly the marks of the tool…the work of the Druids.' Even the OS map of 1854 locates a Druids Circle, and rocks called Druids Profile, and Druids Writing Desk, the latter still named as such.

Sixteenth-century Swinsty Hall is now sequestered in woodland

walk 3

Swinsty Hall & Timble Gill
A tour of haunted places in the Washburn Valley

What to expect: *Fields and woodland, a riverside ramble, a climb to an ancient packhorse track, uneven in places*

Distance/time: 7 kilometres/4 miles. Allow 2½ - 3 hours
Start: Timble Inn, North Lane, Timble, Otley LS21 2NN
Grid ref: SE 180 528
Ordnance Survey Map: OS Explorer 297 Lower Wharfedale & Washburn Valley *Harrogate & Ilkley Moor*
After the Walk: Washburn Heritage Centre, Fewston Church, Harrogate HG3 1SU | 01943 880794 | centre@washburnvalley.org

Walk outline
Pretty Timble sits on a ridge overlooking the Washburn valley. Walk across fields and through woodland to the Elizabethan mansion of Swinsty Hall, overlooking Swinsty Reservoir. Crossing the reservoir embankment, the route follows the infant River Washburn to cross the deeply-incised Timble Gill. A seldom-used path rises steeply through farmland to meet an ancient packhorse track. This narrow track, known as the Bridle Way, re-crosses Timble Gill to climb back to Timble.

Haunted Places of Mystery in the Washburn Valley
A villager, Henry Robinson, amassed a fortune in London by robbing the houses of plague victims. But on his return with the loot, he was shunned by villagers for fear of contagion. Meanwhile, Robinson foreclosed on a loan to the owner of the Swinsty estate, thus acquiring Swinsty Hall in 1596. His troubled spirit still haunts nearby Greenwell Spring…'there he bends and rubs at his ghastly spoil in order to cleanse his gold from any infectious taint'. Another ghost of a murdered traveller inhabits nearby Timble Gill, at the same spot where, two centuries earlier, witches were accused of dancing with the devil.

Local oddity

Common toad

The Walk

1. Facing **Timble Inn**, take the track between houses on the left, to arrive at a junction with a tarmac lane. Turn left and walk out of the village. Just after the last house, bear left off the lane and onto a signposted path between fields.

Keep ahead through field gates across three fields (initially not waymarked), to arrive at woodland and a gated path junction. Keep ahead through the wood, passing a sign for 'Swinsty Reservoir', downhill to a path junction. Turn left and then, after 70 metres, sharp right onto a broad track to arrive at the north side of **Swinsty Hall**.

Of Swinsty Hall, a local man wrote…'many chimneyed, many gabled, grey and grand it stands amid a solitude of woods and fields, a pile of mystery, surrounded by legends'. Greenwell Spring, haunted by the troubled spirit of Henry Robinson, is to the right of the track and next to a small gate into the garden of Swinsty Hall.

2. At the T-junction, with **Swinsty Reservoir** ahead, turn right onto a

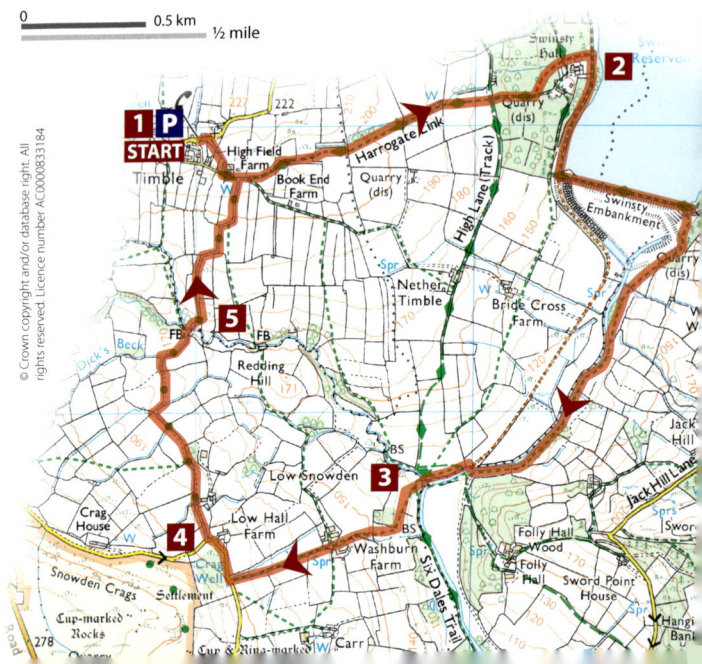

Walk 3 – **Swinsty Hall** & **Timble Gill**

Site of a bloody murder in Timble Gill

broad track to pass below the Hall and continue to the end of the reservoir. Turn left to cross the **embankment**. Just before the Victorian house at the end of the embankment, turn right through a metal gate onto a track passing some pine woodland, which descends to cross the **wall stile** at the valley floor. The path follows the **riverbank** for about 1 kilometre before turning right to cross a wide **bridge** over the **River Washburn**. Turn left to follow the opposite riverbank and after 150 metres cross a **footbridge** over **Timble Gill**.

Further up Timble Gill is the supposed site of the witches of Timble's assignations with the devil.

3. Once over the bridge, leave the river bank and walk up through a gap in the hedge to cross a field and pass below a belt of woodland. The waymarking is poor here, but bear right, uphill, with a beck on the left to cross a wall stile to reach **Sandhill Farm**. Pass through the farmyard and keep ahead uphill to the left of the **farmhouse** and, after 400 metres, reach the junction with **Snowden Carr Road**. Turn right and follow the road round to a left-hand bend at the **Old Granary**.

The Bridle Way enters fields en route for Timble

4. Turn right to leave the road and bear left towards **The Manor House**. Keep ahead through a metal field gate with a black waymarker and into scattered woodland. This path is part of the **ancient packhorse route** from Otley to Timble originally called 'The Bridleway'. At the next field gate, bear right on the old path following an old field wall on the right. It swings right and then left (waymarked), to follow the remnants of an old wall on the left. Look out for a gate with a yellow marker in the corner of the field. Through the gate the path narrows and the ground is uneven. Do NOT take the path signposted up on the left, but continue down **Dicks Beck** to it's confluence with **Timble Gill**.

At this crossing, a man named Wardman was foully murdered by a blow to the head with the butt of a gun. His restless ghost afterwards haunted the scene of his murder, terrifying travellers unfortunate enough to pass that way after nightfall. Villagers were relieved when a local priest exorcised the ghost.

5. This ancient well-worn path continues to wind uphill between fields to reach the lane into **Timble village**.

Writing in the C19th, a villager knew this track as 'the Bridle Road'...'frequented in old

Walk 3 – **Swinsty Hall** & **Timble Gill** ♦ 25

times by packhorses only and towards the brook is deeply worn into the ground…*a very old road and much in the same state as when the witches and their master passed along it to feast in the gill.*'

Turn left and re-trace your steps back to the **Timble Inn** and the end of the walk. The **Washburn Heritage Centre**, in the hamlet of **Fewston** on the far side of **Swinsty Reservoir**, is worth a visit to complete the walk. ♦

The Witches of Timble

Local poet, Edward Fairfax, was convinced his two daughters had been bewitched, and accused several Timble women of witchcraft. In 'Daemonologia' he wrote…'on April 10th 1622 all the witches had a feast at Timble Gill; their meat was roasted about midnight. At the upper end of the table sat the devil, their master; at the lower end the witches who provided the feast'. Later, two 'witches' from Timble were tried but acquitted at the Assizes in York

Winter sun on Fishers Hall in Hackfall Woods

walk 4

Hackfall Woods' follies
Step back in time into an C18th Landscape Garden

What to expect: *Woodland paths, one sustained descent and ascent, superb views over the river valley*

Distance/time: 6.5 kilometres/4 miles Allow 3 - 3½ hrs

Start: St James church, Grewelthorpe HG4 3BW

Grid ref: SE 233 745

Ordnance Survey Map: Explorer 298 Nidderdale *Fountains Abbey, Ripon, & Pateley Bridge*

After the Walk: The Queens Head, Main St, Kirkby Malzeard, Ripon, HG4 3RS | 01765 658497

Walk outline
A short stroll across fields from the village reaches the head of Grewelthorpe Beck and the beginning of this fascinating walk through the semi-ancient deciduous woodland of Hackfall, which clothes the steep ravine of the River Ure. The route follows the top of the woods with magnificent views over the Hambleton Hills, before descending to the riverside to visit enigmatic follies buried in woodland. A steep climb to the last of these follies, Mowbray Castle, completes the walk.

Hackfall Woods
Created by William Aislabie in the mid-18th century, Hackfall is designed as a mixture of the romantic, dramatic and untamed natural world with follies scattered throughout the wood. Painted by Turner amongst others, it became very popular with 18th- and 19th-century visitors, and Empress Catherine of Russia even commissioned a set of porcelain based on scenes from Hackfall. Today, Hackfall is a Grade I-listed 'Historic Landscape Garden', managed by The Woodland Trust.

Hackfall woods

Wild arum

The Walk

1. Take the broad tarmac track across the road from **St James Church**, in between the church **graveyard** and the **Crown Inn**. After 200 metres, and where the track bends to the right, turn left onto a field path signposted 'Hackfall'. The path follows a high hedge on the left to enter **Hackfall Woods** through a wall-stile.

2. Keep ahead to cross a small **bridge** over Grewelthorpe Beck signposted 'Top Pond and The Ruin'. The stone steps to the left give a view over **Top Pond**. Keep ahead signposted 'Fountains Pond and Follies' on a path which contours above the valley. At the next junction, take the left-hand track signposted 'The Ruin and Car Park' which gradually ascends to the edge of the wood, arriving at 'The Ruin', also known as 'The Banqueting House'.

© Crown copyright and/or database right. All rights reserved. Licence number AC0000833184

In the 18th century, William Aislabie, the designer of the Hackfall landscape, brought guests here for alfresco picnics. Visitors could enjoy the magnificent views over the heavily wooded river valley with the Hambledon Hills beyond. The North York Moors are in the far distance. Fifty metres beyond The Ruin is 'Lovers Leap', again with spectacular views. The atmospheric 'Mowbray Castle' (visited later) can be seen framed by trees to the right.

Walk 4 – **Hackfall Woods' follies**

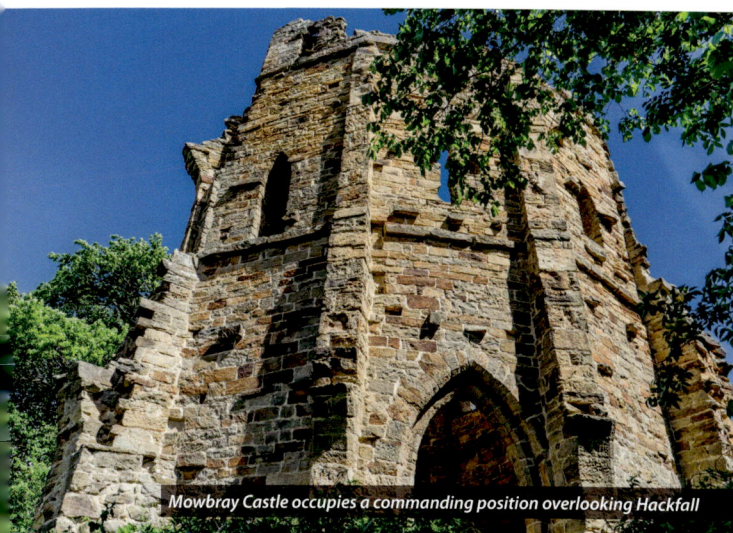
Mowbray Castle occupies a commanding position overlooking Hackfall

3. Keep ahead to the end of the wood signposted 'Car Park' and cross the top of **Limehouse Field**. At the gate, turn right downhill following the edge of Limehouse Field to re-enter woodland near the bottom of the valley. Descend to a path junction, turn right to enter the wood and follow the signs to the 'Viewpoint' on Limehouse Hill.

4. Continue on the zig-zag path downhill to the riverside and through two **stone gate pillars**. Keep ahead and ignore the path on the left to 'Hackfall Garden Feature', to take the right hand path uphill and away from the **River Ure**. After 300m uphill and just before a stream crossing, turn sharply right signposted 'Fountains Pond and Car Park'. After 75 metres pass **The Grotto** with a fine view up to the **Forty Foot Fall** (waterfall) and continue uphill for another 100 metres to reach The **Rustic Temple** and **Fountain Pond** with a view of **The Ruin** on the skyline—a fine contemplative lunch spot.

Imagine fashionable C18th visitors sitting in the Grotto admiring the magnificent waterfall. Historians suggest that the 'rustic temple' had a flagged stone floor and

The Rustic Temple—one of the many follies in Hackfall Woods

that the stone niche at the rear may have housed a religious symbol.

5. Retrace your steps past **The Grotto** and over a babbling **stream** and turn left downhill at the next junction to reach **Fishers Hall**.

The beautiful Fishers Hall may be named after the chief gardener, William Fisher, who laid out the woodland; or possibly because it was used by fishermen in the river.

Just past Fishers Hall, take the steps down to the riverside and rejoin the **riverside path**. Turn right to cross a **beck** and follow the river downstream, the path being boggy in places.

6. After about 750 metres, turn sharp right signposted 'Mowbray Castle', uphill and away from the river, ascending a steep flight of steps for a sustained climb above **Raven Scar**. The path ascends and then contours through **Common Wood** to reach the magnificent folly of **Mowbray Castle** on the edge of fields.

Built between 1750 and 1767, Mowbray Castle is said to be inspired by the semi-demolished Kings Tower at Knaresborough Castle. Set on a rocky promontory, it is best appreciated from a distance, notably from The Ruin across the valley.

7. Passing below Mowbray Castle,

the path gradually descends and, at a path junction, keep left signposted 'Grewelthorpe' to arrive back at the beginning of the Hackfall trail at the head of the valley. Turn left uphill to exit the woods over the wall stile. Retrace your steps across the field path, bearing right where there is a fork in the path. At the tarmac track turn right to walk up into **Grewelthorpe** and complete the walk to complete the walk. ♦

The kelpie of the River Ure

Ever heard of hobgoblins, boggarts, barghests, or kelpies – mysterious and dangerous creatures inhabiting wild and lonely places according to legend? One such tale claims that upstream of Hackfall Woods, weary travellers along the banks of the River Ure might find themselves accompanied by a 'kelpie' taking the form of a beautiful white horse which, if ridden, would gallop off at breakneck speed, and plunge into a deep pool, drowning the hapless rider. So, beware!

The Preachers Cross on the village green, West Burton

walk 5

Knights Templar, Wensleydale
In the shadowy footsteps of warrior monks

What to expect: *Fields, fellside, and woodland. Good tracks throughout. One moderate climb*

Distance/time: 8 kilometres/5 miles. Allow 3 - 3 ½ hours

Start: Village Green, West Burton DL8 4JY.

Grid ref: SE 017 867

Ordnance Survey Map: OL30 Yorkshire Dales Northern & Central areas *Wensleydale & Swaledale*

After the Walk: The Fox & Hounds, West Burton, Leyburn DL8 4JY | 01969 663111 | the.fox.hounds2@gmail.com

Walk outline
From the village green, the route crosses Walden Beck to ascend the western flank of Burton Moor before heading north-eastwards skirting Morpeth Scar giving fine views over Wensleydale with Castle Bolton beyond. Descending towards the valley bottom, Penhill Preceptory is found sequestered in a field surrounded by woodland. The return route contours above woodland to arrive at Morpeth Gate and descend past Flanders Hall to the main road into West Burton.

The Knights Templar
The Knights Templar were founded in France in 1118 to protect Crusaders travelling to the Holy Land. Dressed in white habits with a red cross (the symbol of martyrdom), they became one of the richest and most powerful military orders, known for their religious fervour and indomitable fighting spirit. As their influence grew, money, livestock, and lands, (of which Penhill was but one), flowed into the organisation until they became too powerful and were disbanded by Pope Clement in 1312. Shrouded in mystery, some say that the Knights Templar even found the Holy Grail.

Commemorative stone

Knight Templar

Cauldron Falls at West Burton

The Walk

1. From the **village green**, one of the largest in the Dales, walk down the road to the bottom of the Green and turn right off the road, signposted to the 'waterfall in Walden Beck'.

Cauldron Falls *in its picturesque woodland setting was sketched by William Turner in 1816. There was a corn mill here until the early C20th. There was also an unsuccessful attempt to use the mill to generate electricity for the village.*

Cross by the ancient **packhorse bridge** over **Walden Beck** and, leaving the beck, climb to pass through a field gate. Bear right uphill and keep ahead at a path junction signposted 'Morpeth Scar via Barrack Wood'. Entering the **wood**, turn left signposted 'Morpeth Lane' and follow the narrow path which skirts the western edge of the wood to reach a junction with **Morpeth Gate**.

2. Turn right, uphill, and follow the broad limestone track, known as **Morpeth Gate**, between fields and out on to moorland, passing the imposing **Morpeth Scar** on the right. At a

Walk 5 – **Knights Templar,** Wensleydale

T-junction after the scar, turn left. About 750 metres afterwards, the track reaches the highest point of the walk at a spot height 303 metres. Ignore a right turn and, after another 150 metres, turn left towards the valley on a broad gated track, the entrance to the track being flanked by two trees (Grid ref. SE 038 882).

3. A hundred and fifty metres from the junction, the track bears right, passing a **ruined barn**, and descends on a concrete surface with superb views over Wensleydale. As the track sweeps left, ignore the path to 'West Witton' on the right and soon after, at another bend, turn left off the track onto a grassy path above woodland signposted 'Temple Farm', which descends to a gate into the field in which **Penhill Preceptory** is situated.

To the left of the gate is a **stone marker** *dated 1835 which commemorates the Knights Templar, a few years before the preceptory site was uncovered in 1840. In the field are the* **remains of a small chapel** *with an apse, the remains of an*

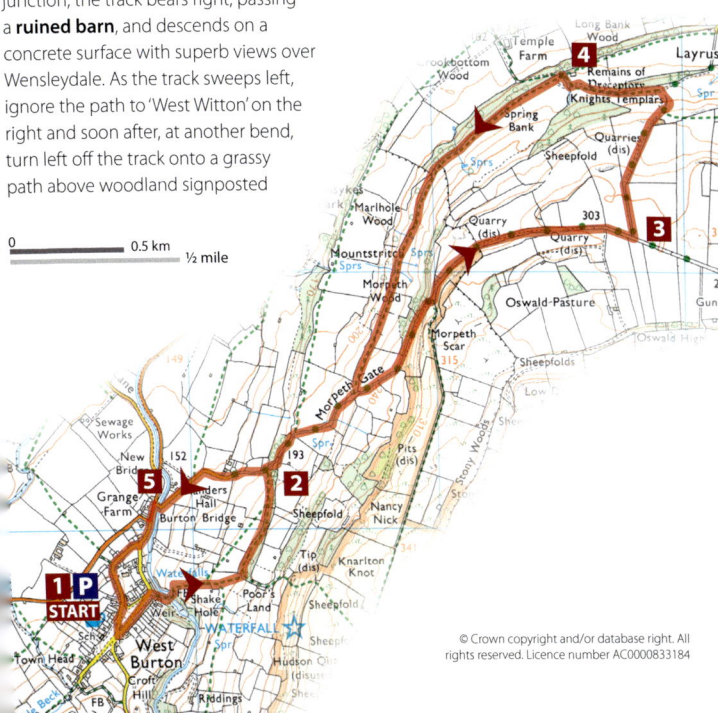

© Crown copyright and/or database right. All rights reserved. Licence number AC0000833184

Penhill Preceptory — all that's left of the Knights Templar in Wensleydale

altar and **three stone coffins**. *The coffins are small and narrow as they contained only the bones of returning crusaders rather than whole bodies. Built in 1202, the chapel was dedicated to 'God, the Virgin, and St.Catherine'. This is all that survives from what would have been the centre of an 80-acre estate with farm buildings, workshops and, of course, a hospital. The site was abandoned in 1312 and by 1324 all Knights Templar property in the area was handed over to the Order of the Knights Hospitaller.*

4. Leaving the **Preceptory field**, pass through two wall-stiles, ignoring the path on the right descending to 'Temple Farm'. The path is signposted 'West Burton 1¾ miles'. The way ahead contours above woodland at the end of which, keep ahead along a wall line on an obvious path until it gently descends to meet **Morpeth Gate**. Turn right downhill and soon the track becomes tarmac to pass the Grade II-listed **Flanders Hall** dating from 1707, and then over a picturesque **humpback bridge** to reach the main road (**B6160**).

5. Turn left and then leaving the main road, turn right, up to the village green and the end of the walk. Unfortunately, there will have been no sign of the Holy Grail on this walk in the footsteps of the Knights Templar!

Walk 5 – **Knights Templar, Wensleydale** ♦ 37

The huge obelisk on the village green is a mystery. Built in 1820 in the shape of a church spire, it is not a market cross, or a butter cross, as the village has never had an official market. Some historians suggest it may be a 'preaching cross', as West Burton doesn't have an Anglican church, being served only by Methodists. The adjacent stocks date from the 1640s. ♦

A Hospice for Knights

Another link to this mysterious brotherhood is at Aysgarth Falls Hotel—two miles to the west of the Preceptory. For centuries, the hotel was known as Palmer Flatt Hotel. 'A palmer' was the name given to a Crusader returning from the Holy land with palm leaves—the emblem of their Order. The hotel had been built on the site of a medieval hospice run by the Knights Hospitaller for the recuperation of returning crusaders.

The secluded entrance to Soska Cave overlooks Littondale

walk 6

Scoska Cave & Littondale

A limestone cavern overlooking bucolic Littondale

What to expect:
Riverside walk and steep climb through woods to a hidden cave

Distance/time: 6 kilometres/4 miles. Allow 2 ½ - 3 hrs
Start: Roadside parking at the Queens Arms Hotel, Litton village BD23 5QJ
Grid ref: SD 906 740
Ordnance Survey Map: OL30 Yorkshire Dales Northern & Central areas *Wensleydale & Swaledale*
After the Walk: The Queens Arms Hotel, Litton, Skipton BD23 5QJ | 01756 770096 | info@queensarmslitton.co.uk

Walk outline

Beginning in the hamlet of Litton, this short walk follows the usually dry riverbed of the infant River Skirfare downstream through some bucolic scenery to cross the lower parts of Scoska Wood National Nature Reserve. Leaving the Reserve, there is a short but steep climb alongside the beck which is the outflow from Scoska Cave, sequestered in the woodland above. After visiting the cave, the return is by green lanes and fields back to the Queens Arms

Crossing the Skirfare

Scoska Cave

In 1905, members of the illustrious Yorkshire Ramblers Club, exploring about 200 metres into the cave, found the skull and several bones of a woman aged about 40, later found to be of Celtic origin, dating from 1,500–2,000 years ago. She had received a fatal head injury from a blunt instrument and had probably crawled into the cave to its extremity and there died. There was no evidence of a burial. Was she a fugitive, or hiding from raiders? Was she an outcast from her community? Or was she murdered? No-one knows ....

Roosting bat

The Walk

1. Facing the **Queens Arms**, turn left and walk up the road for 50 metres and then turn left onto a track signposted 'East Garth'. The track bears right before reaching a T-junction. Turn left to walk beside the **River Skirfare** for 75 metres and then turn right over the river. Fifty metres after the river crossing and opposite a **ruined farmhouse**, turn left into a field signposted 'Arncliffe' to walk down **Littondale**.

Littondale has been settled for thousands of years and the valley sides abound with Anglian lynchets (cultivation terraces caused by ploughing across the slope). The dale was a hunting chase during Norman times and then given to Fountains Abbey in the C13th and used for sheep-rearing. The River Skirfare, a tributary of the Wharfe, runs the length of the dale, but it's upper reaches disappear below ground for much of the year.

2. The way ahead crosses fields to rejoin the riverbank on the left. Take care on this boulder-strewn path. After some 500 metres, the path leaves the riverbank for 400 metres to cross a field before entering **Scoska Wood National Nature Reserve**.

Scoska Wood is a managed ancient woodland clinging to the limestone scars and upper slopes of Littondale's steep valley side. It has been in existence since at least 1500 and is known for its ash trees, grasses, and moth population.

Keep ahead on the level path and, on exiting the reserve, cross a field to arrive at a **ruined field barn**.

3. Turn right, uphill, following a wall with a **beck** on the right.

Mysterious Scoska Cave, remote and hidden within ancient woodland, is halfway up the western flank of Littondale, now designated as a nature reserve.

On reaching the woodland, there is a stile in the field corner. The path up to

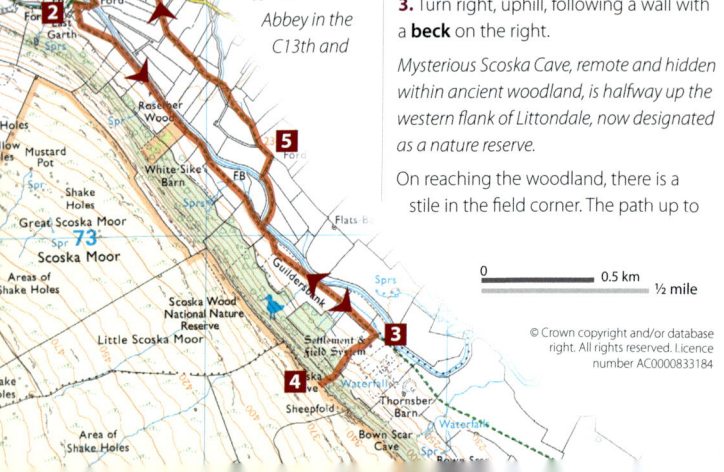

© Crown copyright and/or database right. All rights reserved. Licence number AC0000833184

The first section of Soska's extensive cave system

the **cave entrance** follows the beck, and is steep and difficult in places, but well worth the effort!

4. Taking care on the descent through the wood, retrace your steps back to the barn and then walk upstream, returning through the Nature Reserve. At the far end of the Reserve, turn right to cross the river on **stepping stones**, and keep ahead on a well-made path, with the river now on the left. After some 200 metres, the way ahead turns right, and then left, becoming a **green lane** between walls.

5. At a path-junction, bear right across fields. The route is clearly way-marked until reaching the road. Turn left into **Litton** and the **Queens Arms** awaits to complete the walk. ♦

Cave Archaeology

The Yorkshire Dales National Park is home to half of all the known caves in Britain. Historically, caves have been used as shelters, refuges, dwellings, and as liminal spaces between this and the 'netherworld' for elaborate rituals often associated with burials. Analysis of sediments in caves allows researchers to reconstruct long-lost landscapes, whilst the remains of lynx, hyenas, hippos, rhinos, and so-called 'steppe animals' such as bears, aurochs, deer, and mammoths have also been found.

The Druids Temple is on the Swinsty Estate, near Malham

walk 7

Druids' Temple & Lobley Hall

A wander through a remote estate to an enigmatic 'stone henge'

What to expect: *Wooded valley, fields and country lanes, climb to atmospheric woodland*

Distance/time: 8 kilometres/5 miles. Allow 3 – 3½hrs
Start: Car park at Swinton Bivouac and Druids Temple, Knowle Lane, near Ilton, Grewelthorpe HG4 4JZ
Grid ref: SE 178 787
Ordnance Survey Map: OS Explorer 298 Nidderdale *Fountains Abbey, Ripon & Pateley Bridge*
After the Walk: Bivouac Café, High Knowle Farm, Knowle Lane, Ripon HG4 4JZ | 01765 535020 | www.swintonestate.com

Walk outline

In this quiet and remote corner of the Yorkshire Dales, the route descends into a valley within which a small beck flows from lonely Ilton Moor to the west. A delightful ramble through this bucolic scenery, passing the deserted ruin of Lobley Hall, reaches a country lane and then onto farmland passing some gaunt stands of woodland in the Swinton Estate. The final climb reaches Druids Plantation with its enigmatic 'temple'.

The Druids Temple

This mysterious structure, with its altar or sacrificial stone, its Stonehenge-like monoliths, alcoves, and even a stone table and chairs, leads to a dark cavern at the rear. Inevitably, and given the 'temple's' secluded woodland position, myths and rumours of mystic practices abound, with tales of Druidic worship and the harrowing experiences of those who have spent the night here since it was built in 1820. As late as 2000, having discovered a pig's head on the stone altar, Baroness Masham of Ilton declared 'there *has* been devil worship here'.

Folly in Druids Plantation

Fire ceremony

The Walk

1. Walk away from the road to exit at the bottom of the car park, and bear left below **High Knowle Farm**. The path goes downhill through fields (boggy in places) to reach the edge of the woodland of **Sole Beck Plantation** at the valley bottom. Turn left through a gate to follow the edge of the woods and reach a quiet lane.

The first and last section of this walk follows the 50-mile circular Ripon Rowel long-distance footpath around the lower Ure valley which starts and finishes in the ancient city of Ripon.

2. At the road, turn left for 50 metres and then turn right through a gate with a **decrepit barn** on the right. Follow a broad track alongside **Sole Beck**. Keep ahead on a grassy path, ignoring a footbridge over the beck, to reach the remote and atmospheric Grade II-listed **Lobley Hall** with mullioned windows and chamfered sills. *'NW 1698' is carved over the main door.*

What happened to Lobley Hall is a mystery. Writing about Lobley Hall, one commentator says '… no-one seems to know any of its history, why it was built here and what happened to its occupants…did the family linger through troubled times or

The portal into the hermit's antechamber

was there a moment when they suddenly decided to move on…why didn't anyone move into the house in their place?' One can conjecture, perhaps, that the owners fell victim to the great agricultural depression of the early C19th.

3. Passing below **Lobley Hall**, the path narrows and enters some delightful ancient woodland with bluebells, primroses and anenomes in season. Soon, the way ahead ascends above the beck to leave this pristine secluded wood. Keep ahead and cross two open fields before reaching a quiet lane. Turn left down the lane to reach an old **ford** and associated **footbridge** over **Sole Beck**. Keep ahead on the road as it leaves the valley, ignoring a turn to 'Fearby' on the right.

4. About one kilometre after the ford and where the road turns sharp left, keep ahead on the tarmac track (signposted) leading to **Broadmires Farm**. This route is part of the **Ripon Rowel Walk**. Keep ahead across five fields for just over one kilometre following a stone wall and the edge of **Hall Wood** on the right. The way ahead then leaves the wood and bears left across an open field to reach a signpost for 'Druids Temple'.

Inside the stone circle at the Druids Temple

5. At this point, turn sharp left, uphill, to begin a sustained climb across two fields to the corner of **Broadmires Wood**. Keep ahead with the wood on the left as the path winds up to a red marker and an unusually-constructed **wooden bridge** on the left. Cross the bridge and immediately turn right on a narrow winding path up through a **pine wood** to a wall corner, following a fence on the right.

6. Entering **Druids Plantation**, ignore a track to the right, and keep ahead following a red arrow, with the edge of the wood to the left. The path then bears right ascending gradually to meet a wide track at a T-junction. Turn right to reach the **Druids Temple**, sequestered in the woodland.

At first glance the 'temple' looks like a scaled-down version of Stonehenge, but the focus seems to be the gloomy cavern or 'tomb' with its antechamber at the far end of the stone circle, rather than any orientation to celestial bodies such as the sun or moon. Other clusters of standing stones are found throughout the nearby woodland, which are accessible by permissive paths. A wander through this windswept wood offers superb views over Leighton Reservoir to the west with Masham Moor beyond.

Walk 7 – **Druids' Temple** & **Lobley Hall** ♦ 47

Facing the entrance to the Temple, take the broad track to the left (eastwards) to leave Druids Plantation and then walk back down **Knowle Lane** turning right into the car park to complete the walk.

The **Bivouac Café** is in the farm buildings of **High Knowle Farm** adjacent to the car park. ♦

Druidic Cult

Antiquarians and poets such as Blake and Wordsworth were intrigued by Druidism, leading the landowner of Swinton, William Danby, to design and build 'The Druids Temple' in 1820. Simultaneously, he provided employment for locals at a time of great hardship due to an agricultural depression. For authenticity, Danby hired a 'hermit' to live in the temple for seven years, telling him to remain mute and grow his hair and beard long. He lasted four long years in this role.

Rock art at Hangingstone Woods with Wharfedale beyond

walk 8

Ancient 'rock art' on Ilkley Moor

Discover Bronze Age art on Ilkley's iconic moor

What to expect:
Exposed heather moorland throughout, one gentle climb with superb views

Distance/time: 4 kilometres/2½ miles. Allow 2½-3 hours

Start: Cow & Calf Car Park, Hangingstone Road, Ilkley LS29 8BT

Grid ref: SE 132 467

Ordnance Survey Map: OS Explorer 297 Lower Wharfedale & Washburn Valley *Harrogate & Ilkley Moor*

After the Walk: The Cow & Calf Hotel, Hangingstone Road, Ilkley LS29 8BT | 01943 607335 | www.vintageinn.co.uk

Walk outline

This route provides an introduction to the moor's famous rock motifs—the meanings of which are shrouded in mystery. One writer suggests they…'are a form of sacred art associated with a Late Neolithic/Early Bronze Age cult that only existed for a relatively short period of time'. The walk visits six sites: three on the skyline above the Cow & Calf, two either side of Backstone Beck, and one in Hangingstone quarry. Perseverance is needed to locate the sites.

Ilkley Moor Rock Art

One of the greatest concentrations of Bronze Age rock art in Britain occurs on Ilkley Moor. The most common are cup-and-ring motifs while some have complex patterns containing grooves, ladders, and other elements. What they meant for these ancient people remains a mystery. Could they be maps of the night sky, of settlements, or of springs and waterholes? Are they bound up with rituals with cup-and-rings containing libations of blood, water, or milk? Did they function as territorial markers, or in association with funerary rites or as grave markers? Or, maybe they are just abstract drawings?

'Cup and ring' mark

Cotton grass

The Walk

1. Take the flagged path towards the **Cow & Calf Rocks** and just before the **quarry**, turn left uphill, again on a flagged path. At the top, turn left onto a wide **stony track**. At a track junction, keep ahead (waymarked) aiming for the prominent flat outcrop on the skyline. Bear right at a path junction and continue to ascend to this outcrop. At the top, turn sharp right along the ridge for 100 metres passing a yellow post, to reach the **Pancake Stone** at SE 134 462.

2. Return past the yellow post and, after 10 metres, turn right uphill (southwards) along the line of more yellow posts to reach another prominent outcrop on the skyline.

On the largest of these rocks is the inscription 'WM 1785'—referring to William Middleton, the owner of Ilkley Moor at that time. The moor is now common land.

3. Take the path diagonally downhill for 150 metres, passing a large upright stone to reach the **Idol Stone** on the left—a flat stone with many motifs at SE 133 459.

The design consists of eight cups in two lines of four, and a line of seven cups inside a rectangular carving. A further ten cups, making 25 in total, curve round one end of the rectangular carving. Is there a geometric pattern unlike the seemingly random collection of cups and grooves elsewhere?

Continue down the track for 400 metres to an unmissable

© Crown copyright and/or database right. All rights reserved. Licence number AC0000833184

Walk 8 – **Ancient 'rock art' on Ilkley Moor**♦ 51

Cup-and-ring and other motifs on rock near Backstone Beck

large boulder to the right of the path called 'The Haystack Stone' at SE 130 463.

*The **Haystack Stone** has a large assemblage of cup-and-ring carvings on the top ridge and other motifs on both faces.*

Continue westwards to a path junction above **Backstone Beck.** Turn left, southwards for 200 metres to reach a flat rock to the left of the path with multiple cup features. Immediately after this stone, bear left on a small path for 50 metres, to reach a ruined wall and small enclosure in the heather on the left. (SE 128 462)

This is one end of a semi-circular **Bronze Age wall** facing **Backstone Beck** and incorporating a small enclosure. Its purpose is a mystery but possibly built for the management of livestock. This area, **Green Crag Slack**, has the highest concentration of worked flints on the moor, although no evidence of actual settlement has been found.

4. Continue southwards, uphill across boggy moorland for about 500 metres and bear right to meet a **flagged path**.

This is the main north/south route and former packhorse route across Ilkley Moor.

The Haystack has over sixty cup-and-ring marks, some badly eroded

Turn right downhill and back towards the valley, to cross **Backstone Beck** at **Gill Head**. Turn immediately right, again downhill, parallel to the beck to reach a **seated enclosure**.

This enclosure with letterbox for poems, is associated with the Stanza Stones project. Poems by Simon Armitage, now Poet Laureate, have been carved into large rocks, as part of a Millennium project called 'Across the Watershed'. There is a signpost in the car park to one of the Stanza Stones in Backstone Beck.

5. Continue down the path for about 150 metres with the beck on the right and look out for a flat rock to the left of the path covered in complex motifs of cups, and several deep grooves. This is the **Backstone Beck Stone** at SE 126 463. Continue down the path staying parallel with the beck to a crossing point over the beck.

6. Cross the beck and turn left on a broad path downhill parallel with the beck now on the left. After 100 metres, take a right-hand fork uphill to the left of **Hanging Stones Quarry**. Descend into the quarry bottom and follow the obvious path with the trees to your left. Passing the bottom of a cliff face, turn up left to scramble to the top of the hillock to find the **Hanging Stones rock** at SE 128 467.

Walk 8 – Ancient 'rock art' on Ilkley Moor

There are five sets of carvings on the rock surface. The largest has a deep central cup, double joined arcs and extending grooves, with other cups, rings, and grooves associated with it. Others were destroyed by quarrying in the 1860's.

7. Climb out of the quarry to the top of the **Cow & Calf**, before descending to the car park to complete the walk. ♦

The Ilkley Moor Alien

An incident on December 1st 1987 on Ilkley Moor is one of the country's most famous UFO sightings. A retired policeman walking across the moor met a small dark green figure, with an oversized head and long arms, gesturing at him on the trail ahead. The policeman managed to take a blurry photograph before the creature ran away. He followed but lost it in the fog, before seeing a saucer-shaped craft rise swiftly skywards and disappear.

Looking northwards from the Nine Standards

walk 9

Nine Standards Rigg

A trek on remote moorland to enigmatic stone cairns

What to expect: *Remote, exposed moorland, some peat bogs, breathtaking views*

Distance/time: 8 kilometres/5 miles Allow 3 ½ - 4 hours

Start: Lay-by at the top of the pass on the B6270 Keld/Kirkby Stephen road, 200m to the NW of YDNP boundary

Grid ref: NY 809 043

Ordnance Survey Map: OL19 Howgill Fells & Upper Eden Valley

After the Walk: The Black Bull 38, Market Street, Kirkby Stephen, CA17 4QW|01768 372803| blackbull1963@gmail.com

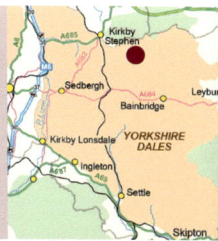

Walk outline

On some of the remotest of Dales' moorland are the atmospheric Nine Standards Rigg. The route climbs steadily to reach these enigmatic cairns, which only become visible within 150 metres of the summit. The return route follows Faraday Gill generally westward, to meet a field wall which encircles the impressive Dukerdale. Follow the wall southwards to rejoin the ascending path and retrace your steps down to the road.

Nine Standards Rigg

The Nine Standards are shrouded in mystery, their age and purpose being uncertain. Re-built over the centuries, they were first recorded 800 years ago but are almost certainly much older, a Bronze Age gold torc having been found in a nearby rock fissure. One theory is that they provided a boundary marker between Swaledale and Westmorland; another is that the Rigg has been a meeting place for Bronze Age herders, nomadic pastoralists, or for long-distance traders—one of the connotations of 'standards' being 'rallying' points. Some suggest they were built by the Romans to warn off marauding Scots. One thing is certain: nobody knows why they are here.

Roofless barn

Carnivorous sundew

The Walk

1. From the lay-by, take the grassy path northwards for 200 metres and at a **crossroads of paths**, turn right to go through a gate on to moorland. Keep ahead across degraded l**imestone pavement** through another gate. Continue on the obvious path north-eastwards through an area of **shake holes**, passing the **head of Dukerdale** and climbing steadily to cross **Rollinson Gill**.

Historically, moors were seen as dangerous and fearful places. Folk talked of 'peg-a-lanterns'—malevolent spirits of the dead whose mysterious lights lured travellers off tracks and into dangerous bogs. Lights were indeed seen on moorland, but a more mundane explanation may be the spontaneous combustion of methane from rotting vegetation, seen less today because of improved moorland drainage.

2. The path winds up the fellside turning generally eastwards passing a **prominent cairn** to reach a path junction and signpost indicating the route of Alfred Wainwright's **Coast-to-Coast** footpath. Cross this, ascending gently until the **Viewpoint of Nine Standards Rigg** (grid ref. NY064824) comes into view with the **Nine Standards** beyond.

In good visibility, the views are stunning; northwards to Cross Fell and Great Dun Fell, south-westwards to Wild Boar Fell and the Howgills, westwards (on a clear day) to the High Street range in the Eastern Lakes, and south-eastwards to Great Shunner Fell which separates Swaledale from Wensleydale. Kirkby Stephen nestles in the valley to the west.

3. From the Standards, take the obvious path down (initially 290 degrees but generally westwards) in the direction of Kirkby Stephen, descending for about

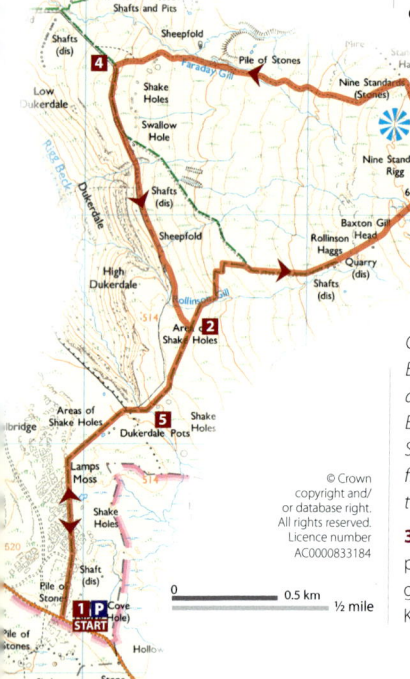

The origin of the Standards is a mystery

300 metres before **Faraday Gill** comes in on the left, and then passing a prominent **large stone cairn**. After the cairn, look for a wall ahead and, leaving the path, bear left to meet this **high field wall** which follows the crest of Dukerdale.

4. Turn left to follow the wall southwards, ignoring a track which leads back up the fellside. The path is little more than a 'sheep trod' in places, but keep ahead beside the wall until the path reaches the head of Dukerdale (over the wall to the right).

5. At the head of the dale, the path meets the outward route. Cross the **beck** and retrace your steps through **two gate**s back to the **B6270** road, to complete the walk. ♦

The Vikings are here

*Norse settlement in the Dales is evidenced by the plentiful names of **landscape features** such as foss (waterfall), ghyll (narrow valley), carr (marshy woodland), scar (cliff), fell (hill), and hagg (woodland on slope). These are all Norse words, as are **built features** such as thwaite (small settlement), garth (small enclosure), thorp (village), gate (street), and laithe (barn). Just look at the OS maps.*

Elbolton Cave—an archaeological treasure trove

walk 10

Elbolton Cave—Hill of the Dead

A sacred hill of the dead, crouched burials, and ancient animal hideaways

What to expect:
Farmland, two picturesque villages and one steep climb. Wildflowers in season

Distance/time: 5 kilometres/3 miles Allow 2 ½ - 3 hours

Start: The Fountaine Inn, Linton BD23 5HJ

Grid ref: SD 997 627

Ordnance Survey Map: Explorer OL2 Southern & Western Dales *Whernside, Ingleborough & Pen-y-ghent*

After the Walk: The Fountaine Inn, Linton, Skipton BD23 5HJ | 01756 752210 | info@fountaineinnatlinton.co.uk

Walk outline
From the village green at Linton-in-Craven, the route enters fields and across well-defined medieval lynchets below Barden Moor. A quiet lane leads to the ancient hamlet of Thorpe hidden in a fold in the hills. Leaving Thorpe, a green lane passes below the southern flank of Elbolton Hill, from which there is a steep climb to the cave entrance at the bottom of a limestone outcrop. The return is a gentle descent across pastures back to Linton.

Elbolton cave: Europe's first mummies?
In Elbolton Cave, three skeletons sat, for almost 6000 years, placed in a crouched sitting position surrounded by a rudimentary wall, until discovered by a local antiquarian, Rev.E.Jones, in 1889. Other finds in the cave included a hearth, crudely patterned pottery, food vessels, worked bone pins and a small bone whistle. Recent analysis has revealed that the three skeletons exhibit canid damage (dogs, wolves) and evidence of excarnation (de-fleshing) before their still-articulated bodies were placed in organic, possibly leather, containers, packed around with stones, and their skulls struck with a blunt object after death! These 'deviant' burials are intriguing?

Cottage plaque, Thorpe

Cave entrance, Elbolton

The Walk

1. From the **village green** in **Linton**, cross the C17th **packhorse bridge** over **Linton Beck** and turn right. At the village outskirts, turn left by **Grange Farm** signposted 'Thorpe Lane'. After two small fields, ignore the sign to 'Threapland' and keep ahead on a broad track climbing the fellside. After 100 metres, cross a stile into a wide field and climb to the left of a large **copse** ahead.

The path crosses a series of terraces called 'lynchets' which were created by medieval ploughing across the slope. Look across the valley for other examples. Elbolton Hill is the large conical hill ahead. It is a 'reef knoll' made up of colonies of coral and algae laid down in a shallow tropical sea, becoming limestone during the Carboniferous period about 300 million years ago. It is one of several in this area, collectively known as 'the Cracoe Reef Knolls'.

2. At the top of the field, cross a wall-stile onto **Thorpe Lane** and turn left. After 600 metres, turn right at a road junction and walk down the lane into the quaint hamlet of **Thorpe**.

The Norse name 'Thorpe' refers to outlying hamlets dependent upon nearby villages. Hidden between the reef knolls of Kail Hill and Elbolton Hill, 'Thorpe-in-the-Hollow'

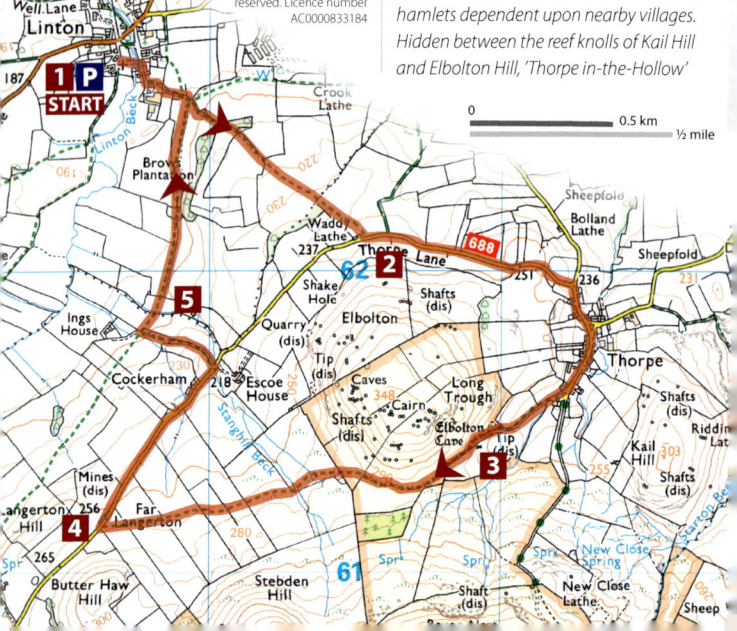

Walk 10 – **Elbolton Cave—Hill of the Dead** ♦ 61

Skulls from Elbolton are in The Craven Museum

was regarded as a safe haven from Scottish raiders in the Middle Ages, where people could hide their livestock. Almost all the houses in this hamlet are listed buildings of historical or architectural interest.

Take the right-hand fork in the road to pass the village green on the left. Keep ahead to walk out of the village and, just before the road gives way to a track, bear right passing a **barn** onto a green lane (signposted), to reach open fell and the base of the imposing bulk of **Elbolton Hill**.

The hill has been the focus of much folk-lore down the centuries. Not only is it known as a sacred 'hill of the dead' since the discovery of the burials, but also as 'the hill of the fairies'. Beware the fairies of Elbolton who, on foggy nights, lead unwary travellers astray with their 'corpsie lights'!

3. This is **Open Access land**. Keep ahead on the grassy track for 200 metres. Turn right into a shallow valley, to climb steeply and cross a large scree of bare rock and rubble. **Elbolton Cave**, also known as '**Navvy Noodle Hole**', is to be found at the foot of the limestone scar/outcrop just above the scree.

Thorpe Lane in high summer

Three bodies, found amongst debris 10 metres into the cave, were placed in an upright, sitting position as though around a crude fire and surrounded by a rudimentary wall. Early Neolithic people believed that by preserving the bodies as skeletal mummies and denying them normative burial rites, the soul of the person was tied to it's bodily home where it could do no harm to the well-being of stock, crops, and people.

Having physical deformities or chronic illness may have identified these souls as 'malign'. The remains of 'steppe animals' including bears were found in deeper sediments. **DO NOT attempt to enter the cave**.

Return to the footpath at the base of the hill and turn right (westwards) to continue on the path passing a **coniferous plantation** on the left. Leaving the hill, follow the line of yellow waymarked stiles over **Stanghill Beck** and across narrow fields to reach **Thorpe Lane** at **Far Langerton**.

The conical hills on the left, to the south of Elbolton Hill are two more reef knolls known as Stebden and Butter Haw Hill.

4. Turn right to walk along the lane for some 600 metres and then, just after a house called **Leaps Ghyll**, and at a dip in the road, turn left on a track signposted 'Linton ¾ m and Threapland 1¼ m'. Just before **Ings House**, turn right at a path junction.

5. Keep ahead across fields to pass below **Brows Plantation** and reach a path junction at a field gate. Turn left passing **Grange Farm** and then right to arrive at the **village green** in **Linton** and the end of the walk. The **Fountaine Inn** awaits. ♦

Elbolton Bear Pot

Deep into Elbolton cave, in sediments below the crouched burials, the remains of what Reverend Jones called 'steppe animals' were found: arctic foxes, reindeers, and several brown bears including cubs. The cave, or 'pot' in the vernacular, was probably used for dens, shelter and hibernation, whilst some of the bones may have been washed into the cave by glacial meltwater at the end of the last Ice Age. The Craven Museum in Skipton displays these finds, including this bear skull.

Useful Information

Visit the Yorkshire Dales
See www.yorkshire.com for accommodation, events, attractions, and festivals.

Yorkshire Dales National Park
Information on what to see and do at www.yorkshiredales.org.uk.
YDNP Visitor Centres are at Aysgarth, Grassington, Hawes, Malham and Reeth.

Tourist Information Centres

Ilkley	01943 602 319	ilkley.vic@bradford.gov.uk
Settle	01729 825192	settle@ytbtic.co.uk
Grassington	01756 751 690	grassington@yorkshiredales.org.uk
Otley	01133 788 875	otleylibrary@leeds.gov.uk
Aysgarth	01969 662 910	aysgarth@yorkshiredales.org.uk
Pateley Bridge	01423 714 953	admin@nidderdaleplus.org.uk
Masham	01765 680 200	info@visitmasham.com
Kirkby Stephen	01768 371 199	visit@uecp.org.uk
Skipton	01756 792809	skiptontic@cravendc.gov.uk

Local Museums

Dales Countryside Museum, Station Yard, Buttersett Road, Hawes, DL8 3NT
The Dales largest and arguably best museum. Archaeology, history and wildlife.
www.dalescountrysidemuseum.org.uk | 01969 666210 | dcm@yorkshiredales.org.uk
Swaledale Museum, The Green, Reeth, Richmond DL11 6TX
Rural history of life and work in Swaledale and Arkengarthdale.
www.swaledalemuseum.org.uk | 01748 884118 | museum.swaledale@btinternet.com
Grassington Folk Museum, Main Street, Grassington, Skipton BD23 5AQ
Period costumes, folk lore, mining and farming. | 01756 753287 | uwmsoc@gmail.com
Museum of North Craven Life, The Folly, Victoria St, Settle BD24 9EY
Cultural and industrial heritage of North Craven. **www.thefolly.org.uk**. |01729 825185|

Weather
Five day forecast for The Yorkshire Dales : 0300 456 0030
www.yorkshiredales.org.uk/visit-the-dales/essential-information/weather

Recommended Reading
North: A Journey through the history and landscape of the North of England, Phil Smith, 2013